Polishing
the Glass
Storm

Also by Katherine Soniat

Starfish Wash-up

Bright Stranger

The Goodbye Animals
(chapbook)

A Raft, a Boat, a Bridge

The Swing Girl

The Fire Setters

Alluvial

A Shared Life

Cracking Eggs

Winter Toys
(chapbook)

Notes of Departure

Polishing the Glass Storm

A SEQUENCE

Katherine Soniat

Louisiana State University Press
Baton Rouge

Published by Louisiana State University Press
lsupress.org

LSU Press Paperback Original

DESIGNER: Mandy McDonald Scallan
TYPEFACE: Adobe Garamond Pro

Cover illustration: Painting by Pierce Landry Jonassen.

Library of Congress Cataloging-in-Publication Data

Names: Soniat, Katherine, author.
Title: Polishing the glass storm : a sequence / Katherine Soniat.
Description: Baton Rouge : Louisiana State University Press, [2022]
Identifiers: LCCN 2021060733 (print) | LCCN 2021060734 (ebook) | ISBN
    978-0-8071-7697-9 (paperback) | ISBN 978-0-8071-7845-4 (pdf) | ISBN
    978-0-8071-7844-7 (epub)
Subjects: LCGFT: Poetry.
Classification: LCC PS3569.O65396 P65 2022 (print) | LCC PS3569.O65396
    (ebook) | DDC 811/.54—dc23
LC record available at https://lccn.loc.gov/2021060733
LC ebook record available at https://lccn.loc.gov/2021060734

for *Tink*

for *Possibility* and *Creation*

Symbols are things thrown against eternity. Forever afterward they bear the mark of that bruising encounter. In other words, things of this world that are drenched with dew of night, impregnated with the energy of revolution, scarred with birthmarks of fingerless midwives—things steeped in auras of intervention.

—Mark Patrick Hederman, from *The Opal and the Pearl*

Contents

Notes

Kuan Yin: Chinese bodhisattva of compassion and mercy.

Egyptian Ba Soul: "The *Ba* was the manifestation of a person's individuality that survives after death. The *Ba Soul* was believed to hover above and guard the mummy—its carefully wrapped body."
—*Book of the Dead* (Tchenena, Eighth-Century Dynasty)

Sanskara: Within Hindu tradition, *sanskara* translates to "he who flows into himself" and thus becomes the perpetual wanderer passing through previous time, again and again.

❧

Polishing the Glass Storm is best read sequentially within each section . . . and also from section to section, as one would read a novel. This approach allows for a dissolving context in which time and space disintegrate on occasion—only to reassemble as a web of the vaguely familiar: Such pattern enables archetype to play an integral role in the movement and arrangement of this manuscript.

*Polishing
the Glass
Storm*

Branches of Birds, Kingdoms That Float

Owl asleep in a willow while the child sits on the levee
with her storybook. O*W*L makes that windy *OWELL*

noise—night bird's name she scratches in the dirt
with a stick. *Branches of Birds: Kingdoms That Float,*

her favorite book the year she turns seven. *For Tink,*
1925, inked in silver on the black page. Almost good

enough to eat—that page with a fat gold moon painted
among bare branches. Her cat, Gray, will want to hear

more about that, even if he never listens when she reads
to him. And any day now, a raft is coming down-river for her,

and whatever else wants to get aboard.   No one can go
home for supper.   The river is there for her daily, but

in bed at night she gets mixed up and starts to miss not
having a mother—the women say "died right after

she was born."   Then Granny had to leave too. Is she
missing one or both of them, and whose slippers are these

her feet kept getting lost in?   In the furry dream   Gray
fades from the levee, then the sky.

҂

Before my mother's looking glass, I hold this photo of her as a child
with the silent gray cat in her lap.   Imagine her   years from then

pregnant after Pearl Harbor—and there I hang   being prepared,
not quite ready to crown—birth muddled by predictions.   The world
at war.

I

I.
small milky formulas

Migration

Watch the patterned weather,
the design of the slow, returning
whale.

Clouds roll by, each shape a whole new
species with no purpose yet in mind.

They cast illusion on rhythms in my whale.

By evening, I want a nocturne on a formal
instrument. Wind blows on the bare branch.

It turns me small,
                    my shadow long.

Bird Gnosis

On the desk, a yellowed photo is labeled
After birth.
      Flesh undone, and there we are
strata on the ridge (huge against the sky)—calcified male
/   female—

pinnacle and gorge   Hungry as lightning

                      ℰↃ

Wasn't it prescient   O, the shadows we could
cast   Sublimely mineral we tried
to bow   (be mannerly) above sea level

Insular   even then—
you   my sandstone porous one   the taller
reminiscence

                      ℰↃ

More and more enthralled, our nerves wound
tight
              And one bird
(or traveling star)   changes the terms of flight
for us   the impossibly erect

(*think   bird   and it sets you free like that*)

                      ℰↃ

Bells from far away suggest another life—
                              after /over/ before
Questions from the ocean   Can love be here but not there?

Touch the place where the heart in me began   No one
asked for a home in space
                    an alpha or omega

                    ❧

Sperm-swaddled egg
        Embryo grown to slip from the groans
of others

What part of us is made to block the wind—
heart medium   brain furrow
midwife palms spread for emergence

Infant balled-up   sacked   then stretched
at birth   Screaming

                    ❧

And don't forget that old *tantrika* who grew worlds
from a single cell
                    What split us in two   from down
to deeper down

Legs jointed   double breasted   and finely sexed.

                    ❧

Before our brief encounter   we were birds
up and out of the sea—
                    hollow bones in the body flying

Cry for me   and suck the salt wind in

Place Where the Wind Is Born

My promise is to stay by the bed, one finger tracing
his forehead into a fountain—up and out of the hospice,
over the garden wall.

He stays and I stay, the loping past, tail to mouth,
circles the room. Feeding. Time twisted about, only hours
left to count forward.
                              Sound disappears. His vocal cords
sigh a bit—the syllabics of this life, done.

Silence enters every muscle. Visceral stillness. His lungs keep
breathing. Little motion but mine that afternoon in the shade-slated
room, the Dalai Lama's chant playing by another sickbed. The fan
moves back and forth, as I blow breath on him.

He receives me like a sail.
Old Fudo, I tell him, purrs at his feet, the ocean vast and clear—
the tiller in his hand. In a strange, fierce tongue I speak
of what is no more.

Not much to let go—diminished relic of a man, something Franciscan
and medieval about him.   By the window Buddha sits

with a load on his jade back.

Kuan Yin Disappears

Why was Kuan Yin and her compassion stolen from his
bedside drawer? Ordinary brass deity beneath some socks

at the hospice.   In war does anyone need to be trained
to strangle or smother? Boots slog up and down, and have

for some time now. Farmland of pigs, babies with the ancestors
set on fire or drowned in the river.   *It's time to spit,* the nurse

says, entering his room. Time to leave *time* alone, I think, and
stay. He cannot smile. Squirrel with full teats scampers along

the garden wall. I almost think I see her young hanging on
for dear life . . . for milk, for anything offered by the vines.

He makes sounds that match and mix and fly by like sparks
from another life.   In the sterile bed he wrestles back

and forth   sometimes with soldiers in a river. Always
in the oldest reaches of his brain.

Dragon Time

January eclipse of the moon in the mountains. Darkness at home in my sheets
by dawn. A wobbly arrangement to start the new year.

                                        End-knots of silver
loosen to constellations—

                       Kuan Yin's foamy dragon,

                           Phoenix startling from the fiery ashes.

And here I am without a clue . . . on top of, beneath and inside
an untouchable scrim of light.

Spelling Backwards

Day begins with wings, peacocks above the water—
shades of other birds in the void.

Pan squats in the garden, tulip between his teeth. He's waiting
for me to dream and cry. Rooster scratching beneath my window.

Teachings again at dawn from the woman in gold: *let the body
lose its head, not the blossom its stem; act from abundance, not lack.*

That said, the words shift to those known to few. My turquoise
from the Andes under the pillow begins with, *Come sleep inside me
and you'll know where you must go.*

Heard in sleep, I'm upended in that row of warehouses, bleating
neema, neema—mantra that reverses to a final

Ameen.

Ameen

is the endnote in Aramaic: *So be it.*
Thus it is.

        Allow the ocean wind to sweep in as no other,
for farther on out it is *afterwards* where you'll be told
never to fill with anything that rose above the rest.

                                Do not flatten
to the low pitch of loss. That's only one of the items made for
fists that clinch above the coast, above glimmery storms in an inlet.
Ivory tusk, parrot wing, and those wild diamond-caked shards of dream.

Terminal creatures we are. But only after the lights blow for a second
time that night, and I've little memory of why or how you left but know
it entered me at a different level. My cat comes to sit still when I speak
of you on the phone.

                    No matter the dimension, it's where you
listen best . . . when neither of us is lonesome or cowardly
in the warehouse district, and we walk on.

(passageway:

some keep a window on the galaxy to wish the lost home. Space neither brokers nor

amends. One girl thinks home her doll cabinet, spirited to the brim. Another pretends

it an airport filled with arms like greeting wings. My game of waiting happens in the hallway

outside the closed-off room. Behind her door change is taking place—anything possible

for my mother's sick and living body

Vanish

Absent, those tissues the year arrived in—months
when I fell behind, then rose
with torch in hand.

The moon is different from the one last year.
                                        Silver,
        how cold the lake looks tonight.

Voluminous wings, these geese fly by to the pier in snow,
that close to my face.

Animus rides low in the birds.
                                Restless vapor,
his summer death more fully absorbed—
no more bargains to strike.

Nothing   but me awake in the mountains.
Pillow for my head,
                    his brain no longer contested.

Commotion over the lake   as if always there'd be a body.

River Dreams

his face—mouth singing that old trance melody. I
wonder if it's Orpheus again, and if he can trust a bit
longer.

Molecular notes   from a head with no body—*Study
the eyes. That kind of detachment wears the soul thin.*

The audience, motionless, lets their faces drop.

(Night-bird cries *whippoorwill, whippoorwill.* Old farmhouse
blows in the field where we slept for a summer.)

Then the jerk to stage-right where I am spotlighted
and naked on the toilet—the kind with armrests and wheels
to support the dying   beside a soiled bed.

It's me on display before what's left of my audience. *Audience
with the queen,* I ask, and they sigh, *what a shame.*   I close my
eyes to go blind—cove where no one ever can find me.

Then that dream collapses into afternoon with me transfixed
in real traffic.
               Alpine waltz drifts from an attic window, and
a guy hollers, *hey lady, don't wait for your friend in the middle
of the street.*   Three-quarter time in the world

unaccompanied.

(vulcan:

nothing comes of my mother's voice. Not a sound from my father. There is no reason

for the timing of war to coincide with birth.   I do not know where others are

as October arrives, and I am a fat and winning child costumed as a pumpkin.

There must have been applause.   Headlights hit my bedroom wall, trying

hard to come home—the radio burning with voices caught in amber

Lake Porcelain

thinned   kiln-broiled   and lazily
cooling   the face composes

so that one night past childhood there'd be recognition
in the eyes of another

Block of clay   that long rendering   (the time it takes
for postpartum flux to slip forward)

Slick blue flesh and the upside-down screams of forced
entry

Headfirst   into the years
unfolding   Dusky clay calendar

Limbs counted and   named   each orifice

Possibility   how did you arrive with one child and a candle

I see through the skin of your canoe—
tincture of lit faces   moving at a tilt
                        underwater

Small Milky Formulas

Child, or whatever form of light you are, why point
to the bottom while the cranes fly high?

Try on your shadow, backlit and blank. Make faces
(nobody sees) at the earth's great ridges.

You know, the ones with certain chin and brow
that we attach to the mountain, then hold fast to

forever.　　　　　Someday you too will find
the limestone caves where the babies were posited.

(small milky formulas)

The changeling's tale: *Daft slip of a girl   She has the remedy:*

Love (bottles of it) she pours through the skin and bone frame

of male famine　　　　　Ruins of appetite hang

by a hair in the wind

II.
(sway:

(another woman:

Peach tree at the center of our yard where deer spat pits as warning. Beyond that, the slope

leads to the ridge where I stop to look down at our house.   Even before us, it had

a cast of its own: tangle of the night-strewn, cellar sprayed with black initials, clothes left

in closets, mattresses tossed.   Standing before a dresser   I saw into another

woman's broken mirror

The Petri Dish Landings

Sleep can't talk but opens the door to a kitchen
where I am classified. The witness.
                                And there is the man,
woman, and their child stranded in familial layers of themselves—
red rising   as in an old darkroom.

But this is the man I knew from the start.   Tonight's experiment
moves his hand for mine by the stove as a petri dish crash-lands
on the stone counter, and the friction between us collapses—
dish labeled, *No touching with fingers.*   *Onion and ammonia*
present in equally combustible parts.

How come no *us*—why this joke on proximity, the way we're
not who we are.
                    Lovers caught at a cave exit.   Shame
on Eurydice   sent back to hell without a word.
Again.

Choke

There's a vortex at the end of any sudden
blue disappearance
an energy that pulls through waves
then grinds the face in sand

Her eyes fill with the ocean
or maybe this is only another
way of seeing the shapes of land
its upside-down dunes with root-hairs
flying loose in the wind

Her birdlike vow   is
to remain above
   it
      but she chokes on proximity
the very the essence of lard

October changes outside to colors that only
resurrect the strangest love-notes ever
painted on her toenails   Each letter
delicately   incised

A Job for the Ba Soul

to broadcast seed across the fields
in time for the Sun God (Ra-e)
to wake for twelve hours,

then sink again into the sleek purse
of the underworld.

For there   dwell Thanatos

and Eros, and every other foiled human experiment.

The book of anything dead leaves secretions in silver: Tarnished
prints.   Journey.
                    Marks the umbilical leaves as karma reattaches.
Is there ever a single point of view for Emerson's OverSoul?

Horizontally   Ba flutters above the wrapped mummy.   It knows
to hold space for the human body.

Sanskara Prayer

Kneeling and truculent in the womb
we are creatures in need—beginning fluctuations out for a sway
in the morning
field.   (damp birth in the dirt)

Come, Aphrodite, save us from earth—sing
ocean scales for a world in harmony
with others.

(Long line of the landed-beasts knocked themselves flat
to discover some bit of empathy for others.)

How do we travel forward with an umbilical, severed, and that
our last road home?

Vertigo of vertical time,   or endlessly scratching claws
across the bottom?

Choice fears   break as waves   along the rocky coast.
There too, tides that move up and down
in and out.

Oily red embed in basalt.   O, pious evening-rose,
the liturgy not sung anymore.

Sister-Feather

Going down for you that last time,
I did not know your name or where

your bones were laid. This circumstance
defined us. *Other Births: Born-alive-but-now-*

dead typed on my certification of being fe-
male, and twenty-three inches long.

Beneath my stats are revelations of my sibling's birth
and death.   How crowded this newborn soul

must have felt, the world already blundering about
at war.   War   I am kin to.

You,   I went looking for but could not pry your
nature loose.   So again I dropped to subterranean pools

where the shades stooped—small ones whose
shapes were incomplete.   Pure and between forms,

how oddly they wobble in water. Then I glimpse
what must be you in the attic window of a bombed-out

house.   Look, here I am—what remains
of a family who rose after dark.   You look absently

my way to where the flimsy faces float, better known to you
than me.   Parts of Eurydice rise, her one good eye and

failed curve of a smile.   Countenance of the blind beloved.
But you, my thought-form, cloud with, *Where is home?*

That's when the wings flap loose and you fly off
into reflection.   Sister-feather I am

to your downy parts   unnamed.

Knees

It's afternoon in Key West and big navy ships
float about the harbor.   Not a gun fires.

My mother and I look alike because we are
in matching pinafores with parts of our name

sewn on. The alphabet is about me when I am
almost four.   Even our hems touch the same

part of our knee. I look at her and wonder
what it's like to be that high above the sand.

I wonder where dead babies end up in the ground.
Some place along the Severn River near Annapolis, I think
my father said, but I forget the rest. Tiny bones
tucked in some sand near the water.
                              But I am going now, flying
north as any child can do—up the coastline, over lighthouses, graveyards
and sandboxes on the ground.
                              I'm on my trip away from my little mother
and that place called *stinky fishing village.*   A man yelled those words last night
when I had on my dress, its hem touching my knees that were like, or maybe
were, hers.
              I don't know what belongs to who or where anybody's going.
I am happiest in our mother-daughter clothes.   Like being a fish looking
for others   then comes a swirl of every fish ever, and lost
babies in sand.

Plate Tectonics

Cool   the wet   and pluvial

shaggy natured   the clouds roamed

Long before glyphs or human inflection
those chilled vapors hung

Such a gentle watering after ice dragged and puckered
the earth

Fault lines rattled from the inside out

Plate tectonics cracked the lithosphere
Orogeny   Not to blame those great disturbances named the mountains
Four months old   I did not watch my father open the door to leave for
wars lost on land and sea

Blank calendar, blank check for *gone for years at a time*   Broken bodies

categorically crammed under   It's the unknown I miss
Never am I missed   in love as I am with absence

For Sweet Dreams

Crimson with rash, I'm in bed in a hotel, my box of blue
capsules for sleep labeled: *por sueños, dulce y tranquilos*

beside me. Swallowing three with red wine, I doze off
to wander from door to door calling—*I'm here for sweet dreams*—

until a figure ushers me into the room where you're dying. Winter here,
embers smolder in the grate.   The scarlet rug with a bear woven at its center
covers you, almost up to the eyes—as if I need a reminder in this room with your
white metal bed on wheels.

Again, I insist that I've come only for dreams, knowing that when you're gone,
part of our darkness will be complete.

From down the hall comes the smell of stew, that domestic porridge,
and I want you, the father of my children, not to die. I promise to stay on the path
with our basket of food as slowly you rise from bed

to hold me from behind. With your hands on my stomach, you say
we're headed home, and this time it feels right to be going, sundown
in a gold winter day.
               Then, as if doused,

                    that dream goes black,

                         blank—

                    my basket stone-heavy
                    and empty.

(sway:

locomotive lights make the willows flare and go out on the far side of the levee

where catfish suck the marrow   toes   and little fingers of all that enter   Once

a suicide flashed from the bridge in car headlights   My cigar box of trinkets

holds that photo and clipping   One whole woman like that in midair

III.

collections of war

Hour of the Baboon

Wolf-moon rising. Pack of we-shalt-eats
howl with the wind, then overtake the sled

to chew fingers from a man's hand (sinful little
fingers at that). Ancient biblical parts made to be

imagined but hidden from view. Scripture drools and rolls
over for here comes the parade of our twitchy regressions

through sex, greed, and wars until it's back-to-wolf—with You,
O, upright one, who in most instances thinks of itself first

and foremost, especially while writing poetry. Yes, you over there
with the quick-silver tongue and stacks of fat pink erasers, always

wanting one more Eternity just to get it right.   Check out this
Forever and a night—those demonic spaces between 2 and 6 a.m.

when screaming *bloody murder* just gets screamed some more
while men leap from the flaming tower. Chop go croc's antique teeth,

practicing.   *Hour of the Baboon,* one sage named it.
Cocktails at dawn with the red-bottomed,
and mad for more.

War Memorial

The day they put you back in the hospital ward,
you told the janitor how to be in five places at once
but only after he discovered you'd invented the plastic
garbage bag, so everyone at the nurses' station was convinced
you were a millionaire and me the prettiest woman this side
of the toilet down the hall—because you said so and they
liked you, and I liked them.

In the parking lot that morning I held a blend of carrot juice to the sun,
and the man in the next car whispered to his wife, *she must be European*—
something highly suspect in that smoothed concoction of carrots, ginger,
and celery spun with light.
                              Returning to those places you lit out for
with your ochre robe flying.   Exact locations as inexplicable
as the old fox koan.
                   In your hospital bed, you try hard to show me
what is wrong. *Like this,* you manage   palms missing each other.
Split line.   Your never-meeting hands   says it all.

Farfetched Has Glass Doors to See Through

The gray cat swipes at her ankles, licks hands, and leaves planning behind.
Song becomes amnesia . . . convoluted moments when death jumps in
(and she'd have dropped to all fours to coax his essence back).

What if she'd not spotted love being born behind glass in Dresden during the
war.   At twelve, she was sure that man and lady figurine both placed their small
pink tongues in each other's
mouth, kissing.

She sang to them in German (the country in which those two concocted
a life of most-favored-china status, and that kind of crazy
old-world stuff).
                              In those days families shifted about grimly and her father
kept flying into her room saying she'd always be his favorite in their tree
full of owls.

(earth:

if it's not the sea that shines, it's showers on a river that slips birdlike through the tropics.

Parrots tilt brilliance above the fern.   A nod to afternoon in the leaves, to feet

padding below.   Boys glide the ocean, birds the air.

It's childhood or better for a long while before hand and eye come together

to crush the horizon

A Curious Few

At sunset she reaches to touch the mountain lion before it leaps
to the next outcrop of rock.　　　　　Remember when life
returns, possibility frightens more than the corpse.
Hold the energy animals wait inside—quiet gold blur on the ridge.
This too soon will shift to a different meaning.

                             ℰⁿ

Why is it only when the million parts pull together that the human
gains a sense of itself?　　Prof. Eaglesmith ponders this fact at his desk
down the hall. And also how inexplicably some people get along
with the symptoms of this life, while others succumb without
trying.　　　　　Propositions, proposals come and go. If it's
for memory, study the songbird. But what of the man with fewer
thoughts in his head each day?
　　　　　　　　　　　　Eaglesmith listens after dusk for plangent
plainchant of the humpback whale.　　Behind the curtain he stretches,
then falls to his knees for a willowy plunge through clownfish on his way
to the ocean floor, then maybe beyond.

                             ℰⁿ

She loved his hands though he would leave in the next measure of time
which would make her wanting for seasons ahead. His words hardly
came anymore. But something slapped around like a heart at the bottom
of a boat when she asked, *Do you want me to stop touching you?* From no-
where came a formally managed, *No.*　　She squeezed his arm and
turned away like a deceased ghost, so hard was it to walk away on a day
that to most was like any other.　　Through the door evening came
to stretch her across the hospice　　　　　then farther.

As a child she imagined death and blindness's pale flicker as the same.
Recall the song of the empty room—litany thrust against shades.
The end to definition.

                    Without a word   Kuan Yin leans in beside him
with her seven yellow feathers of compassion.   She listens for his least
inhalation. How does breath return again and again in the humid decathlon
of a jaguar   panting?

Pedagogy

Who knows how insistent the mind can be
about its need for words, syntax, and sudden flashes

of plot?

An hour a week to work on writing a silly book? Ego always wants
a pinch more, eh?   : :   Another man's way of thinking.

And how many pictures could be taken as Teacher pinned
this man to his past?   He stuck him there, photographing
each grimace, until Student

fell to pieces.
                    What good came from feeding the sick
man pints of ice cream to keep on weight, to keep him alive
in his hut behind the big zendo?

Then the man with the robust brain was doing it again: aspirant
up to the chin in hospice sheets.
                                        See this frowning male and his mind
circle the bed, taking more close-ups
of a dead man's face?

Promises of More

During the Paschal holy week of the Lamb,
a disease that had no name ate away his edges

as she sat in the courtyard on a bench and smiled intently
at the sky

Solar pulse going   then coming

The law of attraction is not the law of recovery   of obtaining and
holding onto a man about gone
                                        Where is her handlebar (for she's flying
off-center in the new spring grass)   to make a hard right turn out of
April   May   and those first three days in June
when he proved himself no more

(stick figures:

the outbreak of order was over. Time to move as far as spring would take her, water

streaking every window. Time to carry things from the house. All day the storm blew. She

was stealing herself away, sack of pond flowers on her back, wooden furniture carted off

like stick figures to a truck. Lightning whitened the pond, the hills. By night the walls were

bare, and rain poured down on what was done

And Done Again

Promised, no illusions until that plan rolls over, burying its head
in the dirt. And still the grit's flying as the train derails, maybe loses
some wheels, and we're face to face on the earth.

                                   Sudden and fresh and
whole, or maybe headed that way. Take a breath, my love, before you mix
with me for already I am calling myself, *spirit estranged* (tincture-of-leopard),
and you quickened *thrall of red weather.*

We sink into our sleepy animal brains to keep winter away. Story
recedes. I open my eyes, that certain we're part of the wind. Then
it arrives—tardy, stern, and sniffing first my hand then yours
for direction, for some signal to erase even the coils of DNA.

It wants to stand for us. It stands above as you say *I want this,*
and grand dunce that I am thinks, *of course I am this female
entity most desired beyond now.*

42

Lyric Runes

Blindfold her please, so she'll not confuse herself with the eyes of another.
Wasn't there a big bright moon over the potholed parking lot?
Hush her Orphic stretch for meaning.   No nest of vipers
yet.

There was   this timeless churning of Etheria where the elementals
gathered and raged and bred   then took it too hard.

That's how the narrative goes (that went)   the way two charmed figures
demanded more and more of the dark. The company they kept with masks
that offered escape.
                    Who thought that in one cockeyed instant the point
would fall away   and   whatever two can do   they did

Incision below the belt

[a wet blue spiral]

(butcher:

letting herself go to sleep in an empty house was hard   Like rolling over into the sunken

hollow.   Morning, trucks came fuming.   That burlap sack still wriggling downstream

while Mr. Hatch hid things under his butcher apron . . . watching her upside-down

in a garbage bin behind his store after celery tops for her rabbit's breakfast

Triptych: Collections of War

i. ThinAsaDime

Fish set out for the cat, she drifts off at midnight.   Everything
as slippery as eel in the marsh.   She stalks murk (and mirror-sheen) of the departed.

Sitting cross-legged in the reeds   she's the posture of patience   of winter.
Her inner gaze goes to the war where a soldier lets his surname drop—*ThinAsaDime.*

Without stomach, brain, or heart, he's part of a disorganized lot. The kind
at large   when nothing weighty is allowed through the gate.

Human-been-there-done-thats   (with coins for teeth
to push the grease from each finger),

ii. matter

She changes to a limousine—sleekest of the black vehicles.   Hard capsule to swallow
(even if she's inside).   The sky's   bulbously swollen   Cars blunder about

without headlights.   And all she can do is say, *Why this?*   *Why that*
total eclipse of the moon?   Was darkness the first sign of dread ever?   Streets crack.

Animal tails wave from a dumpster.   Too much extinguished   Extinct   (energy
 knots her pelvis).   Bomb #2 flourishes in florescent-green plutonium.

Second nature (hers) hears the great wheel grind to a halt.   Ready to venture,
Is this it ?   *This is it,* she says,   *war thickens the earth*

Foresight   hindsight—none of that matters.

iii. breathless

in sloppy red oils are the creatures left trying.   Hieronymus Bosch slumps
(even after all that cross-eyed wisdom from the elders).   Alarm blasts her

awake. The mind stutters, *Now   get up   go find those with the motherless,*
unfathered auras : :   or maybe just look for the young stationed at four corners

of the roof. Nothing there seems in denial (or appears flatly soulless)?
Into body cavities she peers   for hearts plump enough to fit in her palm

(and indeed each of them has one).   *Why this roof garden*   she whispers
as brilliance busts up the stars.

All a roof can do is crush you and your not-too-swift lineage
from butchers   (a voice says)   *to the sad clairvoyant.*

IV.
polish

Fire Devotion

Touch the secret where
the heart in me began,
                                    cells
in the amniotic pool.

A startle, perhaps, to a certain way of thinking—
the schism of another

                        breaking through.

Curled in liquid, the spine perfected.   Fetal and
blind,   I bow.

Private   those stations of the fire.

            And ahead, that promiscuity called November.
Naked limbs.   The orifice.   Sap configuring . . .

the same over

and over.

The same as ghost strata in the canyon, and those mating
hawks each spring—
                        shadows over doorways.

Our cold chamber, space.   Friction and flint,
darkness set on fire.
                        Slowly sound arrives for *only* and *once.*

Solitary.

The intimacy of time.

In Bed at Night

In my mother's house there was no heart.
In my mother's heart she was always looking
for a home.
          I threaded stories of her, ones neither
of us had heard. Soft ones with feathers
at the bottom.

When my son had a daughter, she came into this blueness
knowing details with a past.

In bed at night playing puppets with the covers, she had
the smallest one whisper, *You know, there's so much sadness in this world.*
She was three, and I almost didn't hear that.

It was dark in the room, and inside her head.   She thought in stride
with nothing—humped-up sheet, her cave in a city on earth
that just might go away.

The Book of Healing

Saint Teresa speaks on Facebook, her words
for this spent holiday—on giving and humility, and
how nothing is too small.
Gifts there before species were tagged and counted.

                                                 Before us,
the void was nameless. And there was no greater or less than.
Silence was with the stars. Without plans, each had its place—
the cave, those at home in their animal skins.

But you are uncovered on the medicine bed   White bear
nailed to a wall. Fire voices roar beyond thinking. Tundra wind
and light whips your body.

We Stand Face to Face: Singing Pilgrims in Sparkling Bearskin

Smell of bear   barks in the forest

My body has a hole behind the heart
the lock in front—measures of
animal-dampness breathe in between.
Bear blue eyes hold me to dream—
that close, two paws on my shoulders.
Such weight   means   *don't move*
but I do   and bear grabs my hand
in its teeth.   This part of me never
will be again—that line of thinking—
as its tongue relaxes to licking, and
we get on fine in the dark. Restlessness
spent   warm saliva might well create
my next home. Freshly skinned and
slick   I am all over again

Slowly   a dead body heaves down through the branches

Feather Weight

> Birdlike, Ba Soul embodies the human heart in the nether
> world where it gives evidence for, or against, its possessor.
> During this ceremony (Weighing of the Heart) this organ
> should weigh no more than a feather.

After a difficult period, the man argues with his Ba Soul about the merits of life
as opposed to the uncertain nature of life after death.

In the end, Ba Soul advises the man:

Desire me here (in life) and reject the West (land of the dead). But also desire
that you reach the West when your body is interred . . . for then and there,
I'll alight to watch over you. We'll make good harbor together until dawn.

(Queen Karma:

builds kingdoms on the stonewall at three years old   Twig huts   chipped-glass

fence of amethyst and blues   Most rainy afternoons the plum dress in her

mother's closet served as a roof for yet another home—like crawling in space

after the darkest day

Blush

Jyotsana means "moonlight in the forest" throughout India
so she plays her queen of diamonds on the green tile table as light
rises way off shore—gold-spotted leopard at dawn. Heat moves
slowly on the far side of the earth.

Fish flicker in the bay. By evening she asks the man to meet her
at the cave opening. He talks about his plans being worldly (definitely
other than hers), and how he must fetch someone who flies by air.

A peacock, she bets, knowing this will not be the end of her lust
for birds.   To confuse, she asks if he can guess (which he can't)
what makes her sing in her sleep for that is a clue to her dimension.

Other answers could be variables on that feeling below the navel
when the grass tickles as she crawls toward the Cave of the Loon.

With such consummate wilderness in mind the woman of diamonds
shakes her facets loose—hundreds of them—and the sun turns away.

(child bed:

Walnut Street ends at the bend in Broadway. That's where her first home stands, along

with the child bed, as they called it. Small mattress curls like a feather to the wall that curves

with Broadway and the levee as it follows turns in the rising, falling Mississippi. Her body

trembles as trucks take a swing in the road, braking hissing with deliveries for Hatch's

Meat Market

Peaches

There was a time when they were moments into a new temporal pool,
                    and afterwards she walked into doors,
trying to find her way to the closet. She had a thought
and lost it,

                    sensing what it was to breathe the island-nature
of the mind.   She straightened the bed and saw indeed she had on
        clothes, so proceeded to the mainland where grocery shelves
decisively loomed so that she might select from gaily colored boxes

                    and glazed bottles—thus receive good-woman marks
for doing such.   But something else held on.
She felt dissolute and unaware. Peaches changing shades
on her windowsill.

Consider How They Grow

Declaring her heart a lily, a koi, an integral organ of earth, she turned
to the elders who stared as if she were mud   for they ranked themselves

monolithic and more complex.   The oldest entities around.   Of course
she puzzled over such thoughtless insult to the mountains with their mineral-

riddled status.   Like juts on Mount Rushmore, not one of her guys would
crack a grimace. Some dangled dogma, others roped buzzards to friends

at the summit.   Not one knew the differences between *spin*
and *toil*—surface dervishes spin the lilied field . . . then the toil from

down to darker down.   Vertical sickness.   Not a soul left
to copy or infiltrate.   Silhouettes on the ridge hold the posture of dawn—

hearts pressed skyward.

(refusal:

Iris recalls the missing petal—pressed to a glow, it's an energy that won't succumb

to circumstance. The twilight of what left, rising and eerily real. No future like that

of the fresh survivor   no past like that of a relic—dead pheasant shoveled from

the road, but for one wing prone and blowing in my headlights. Another refusal

to leave at once and go quietly

The Time It Takes

Buddhism holds that after forty-nine days,
the deceased begin to transition.

He liked the time it took to read a book
and wanted someday to write one.

The doctor had to considered words carefully before saying,
An utmost need to communicate comes with speechlessness.

I do not recall her name.

Weeks into wishing, I learn to see what's absent
with sheets on a moonlit puppet.

Solitary pear, my prop.   Pollen trails the lost around.

Two of us in your hospital room that afternoon: you mindless
of me or who I ever was.
                    Tonight, I knew you'd come, the cicadas
that loud.   It just takes time to make it up the tangled ravine,
and into my room

Apostrophe

i. *he*

Gone   our night by the lake
along with my cockeyed guesses

You   live on essences

Wrapped in my own summer death—I hesitate, planting mirrors
of recognition   between spheres

across species   and inside flashing weather

Want more than a pier in the snow   Wild geese

call   Flapping bright bird with a future

ii. *she*

Afterwards   nothing held me to a bed
to the figure called woman

Come   lie down beneath me   on top of
whatever else breathes in this world

Touch between the lines

Kuan Yin's dragon decanter of blood
oranges   our bedside elixir

No interruption   You fade
with the mind   and myth of the mind

and any thought of what comes after

Mummy Tales

from Horus of Nekhen (c. 3100 BC)

Your life happens again—for the Ba Soul guards your divine corpse.
Ba and the *Akh* (the Spirit) join as one as you move forward by day
with your body, and return each evening to your wrapped mummy.

A lamp is lit for you at this depth until sunlight shines again on your heart,
when you shall be told: *Welcome, welcome again into this, your house of the living!*

Polishing the Glass Storm

Cryptology   speaks (~ * / < \ ) in gold and silver

Coded shapes   masks   to hide behind
while being presented with (or present in)

a new life

(Frequencies buzz with interpretation
Indeterminate ruminations)

Breathlessness   of the first   fly-away-or-stay   thought-question
as Eros magnifies heat enough   to scorch the brain
(swoosh)

Bees in a crazed terrarium—swarm creatures   all

(polishing the glass storm)

Why so . . . Ba Soul's job it is to hover speechlessly
above the strapped imperial mummy—

myth Ba erects   skeletal joke of naked-as-you-go   poor
old kings and queens   relentlessly tied and bundled

The body counts   (forwards and back   it does)

Numbers count too—
                            rigmarole of forever   then those endless days

Pronouns: the *he/she/it/* and *they* of it   and of course the *royal we*
who cross every boundary and will not be set aside

SHUT   a directive lovers and young souls deny

Acknowledgments

Many thanks to the editors of the following journals and anthologies, in which the poems listed first appeared, sometimes under different titles: *Absinth Poetry Review:* "*Sanskara Prayer*"; *Asheville Poetry Review:* "Another Woman," "Butcher," "Child Bed," "Earth," "Queen Karma," "Refusal," "Stick Figures," "Sway," "Vulcan"; *Bayou:* "Apostrophe"; *Citron:* "Lake Porcelain," "Small Milky Formulas"; *Connotation Press: An Online Artifact:* "A Job for the Ba Soul," "*Ameen,*" "And Done Again," "Bird Gnosis," "Fire Devotion," "Lyric Runes," "Polishing the Glass Storm," "Promises of More," "Spelling Backwards"; *Hotel Amerika:* "Apostrophe," "Blush," "Dragon Time," "Farfetched Has Glass Cabinets to See Through," "Kuan Yin Disappears"; *Intimacy* (anthology): "Bird Gnosis"; *It's All Relative* (anthology): "In Bed at Night"; *Mad Hat Review:* "Choke"; *ONE:* "The Time It Takes"; *Pedestal:* "Peaches"; *Posit:* "Consider How They Grow," "Hour of the Baboon"; *Prairie Schooner: (Water Fusion #6):* "River Dreams"; *Saint Katherine Review:* "A Curious Few," "Pedagogy"; *Southern Poetry Anthology, Volume VII:* "Bird Gnosis," "Fire Devotion"; *storySouth:* "Triptych: Collections of War"; *Superstition Review:* "Knees," "Sister-Feather"; *Thinking Continental: Writing the Planet One Place at a Time* (anthology): "War Memorial"; *Tiferet:* "Branches of Birds, Kingdoms That Float," "Migration," "Plate Tectonics"; *Turtle Island Quarterly:* "The Book of Healing," "The Petri Dish Landings," "We Stand Face to Face: Singing Pilgrims in Sparkling Bear Skin"; *World Poetry Portfolio #60:* "Bird Gnosis," "Fire Devotion," "Place Where the Wind Is Born."

CPSIA information can be obtained
at www.ICGtesting.com
Printed in the USA
BVHW052227151022
649558BV00004B/303